Americans All biographies are inspiring life stories about people of all races, creeds, and nationalities who have uniquely contributed to the American way of life. Highlights from each person's story develop his contributions in his special field — whether they be in the arts, industry, human rights, education, science and medicine, or sports.

Specific abilities, character, and accomplishments are emphasized. Often despite great odds, these famous people have attained success in their fields through the good use of ability, determination, and hard work. These fast-moving stories of real people will show the way to better understanding of the ingredients necessary for personal success.

BANNEKER's
ALMANAC,
For the YEAR 1795:
Being the THIRD after LEAP YEAR.

CONTAINING,
(Befides every Thing neceffary in an Almanac,)

AN
Account of the Yellow Fever,
LATELY PREVALENT IN PHILADELPHIA;

WITH
The Number of thofe who DIED, from the Firft of
Auguft till the Ninth of November, 1793.

# Benjamin
# Banneker

## ASTRONOMER AND SCIENTIST

by Margaret Goff Clark

illustrated by Russell Hoover

*GARRARD PUBLISHING COMPANY*
*CHAMPAIGN, ILLINOIS*

*To my father, Raymond F. Goff,*
*the first to encourage me to write.*

## Acknowledgments:

For his generous help and advice I wish to thank
Silvio A. Bedini, Assistant Director of the National
Museum of History and Technology, Smithsonian Institution.

I also wish to thank Mrs. Maurice Zackheim, Assistant
Director of the Niagara Falls Public Library, and the
reference staff of the library for helping me to obtain
early authoritative material on the life of Benjamin Banneker.

## Picture credits:

Bettmann Archive: p. 2 (almanac)
Culver Pictures: p. 78 (top)
Schomburg Collection, New York Public Library: p. 2 (portrait), 84
I. N. Phelps Stokes Collection, New York Public Library: p. 70, 78 (bottom)

# Contents

# 1. Can Thee Read, Benjamin?

"Wait till you see our colt!" five-year-old Benjamin Banneker cried as he ran into the log house where he lived.

The day was warm and Ben's legs and feet were bare. The boy came to a halt right in front of his grandmother, Molly Banneker, who was sitting beside the smooth-scrubbed table. It didn't seem strange to Ben that she was white while he and his little sisters were black. She loved him and he loved her. That was all that mattered.

"The colt's wobbly," Benjamin went on, "but he's standing up beside his mother. Pa says I can help—" He broke off as he saw that his grandmother was holding a well-wrapped package in her lap. "What's that?" he asked excitedly.

Molly Banneker's blue eyes glowed. "Guess what it is! It came all the way from England!"

Ben lifted the heavy package, but he could not guess what was in it. Eagerly he helped to remove the wrappings.

"A book!" he exclaimed in wonder. "Is it yours?" He had not seen many books, as in 1737 they were too costly for poor people to own.

"Yes. It's a Bible. I sent for it because I want to teach you to read."

Ben put his hand on the thick cover. He ran his fingers across the raised letters that as yet meant nothing to him.

Slowly he opened the book and looked at the lines of print that covered the pages. Excitement grew inside him like a bubble ready to burst. The printed pages were mysteries to him, but soon he would know the meaning of those strange marks. Someday he would read this big book all the way through.

Sitting down beside his grandmother, he said, "Let's start now."

Outside, the hot Maryland sun shone on the small hillside clearing where the Bannekers' one-story log house stood. Little Minta, Ben's baby sister, was on the doorstep, playing with her cornhusk doll. Robert and Mary Banneker, Ben's father and mother, were at work in the tobacco field not far away. Ben had planned to go with them, for even at five he knew how to help. But now he had forgotten everything, even the new colt.

He pointed to one of the gold letters on the cover of the book. "What's that?" he asked.

His grandmother smiled at his eagerness. "That's a B. It's the first letter in the word Bible. It's the first letter in Benjamin and in Banneker, too."

Ben traced the B with his finger, fixing its shape firmly in his mind. Then he went on to the next letter. Soon he could read the word Bible. When his father and mother came in for the noonday meal, Ben did not want to stop studying the new book.

Every day, with the help of his mother and grandmother, he learned a few more words. His father had never learned to read, but he took pleasure in listening to his son.

"Maybe Benjamin will be a preacher," Molly Banneker often said. "He's a bright boy, and we must give him all the learning we can." Her eyes were sad as she looked at her grandson. "It's hard for a black boy to make a place for himself in the world, but somewhere there ought to be some important work for Ben to do."

As soon as Molly heard that a school was opening nearby, she declared, "We'll send Benjamin—he's six, and that's old enough to start school. I'll pay his tuition. I saved some of my sweet potato money."

On the first day of school Benjamin scrubbed himself until he shone and put on the new homespun shirt and pants his mother had made for him.

The school was not far away, but Ben was glad to have his mother go with him that first morning. Grandmother, carrying the baby in her arms, walked with them as far as the edge of the clearing.

From there, a path led into the deep woods. Most people in Maryland traveled on such trails, for there were few roads. Narrow rays of sunlight came through the leafy branches of the huge oaks, maples, and beeches that lined the trail. Something rustled in the undergrowth, and Ben opened his eyes wider to see through the gloom. A squirrel scampered across the path and up a tree.

The school was held in the home of the teacher, a kindly Quaker gentleman who met his pupils at the door. He had a paper in his hand on which he wrote Ben's name and where he lived.

"What is thy birth date, Benjamin?" he asked.

"It's November 9, 1731," Ben answered promptly.

The teacher took him into a clean, simple room and showed him a bench where he might sit. Several other pupils were already in the room. Ben noticed that most of them were white, but two were black like himself.

As Ben was one of the younger pupils, he was placed in the beginning class with three other boys. They began to study the letters of the alphabet. The four boys were given two hornbooks to share. The hornbook was a piece of wood shaped like a paddle. On it was pasted a sheet of paper which contained the alphabet, a list of numbers, and the Lord's Prayer.

Over and over the teacher pointed to the letters and read them aloud. Over and over the four boys repeated them.

"Now thee study the letters while I teach the older students," the teacher said.

Ben liked the Quaker way of saying *thee* and *thy* instead of *you* and *your*.

To him it sounded like the language of the Bible.

Quickly he read the letters over again. He read everything on the hornbook. Then he listened to the older pupils.

He was startled to hear his name.

"Master Banneker," said the teacher sharply. "Pay attention to thy work!"

Ben was too shy to say that he knew the alphabet, so he bent his head over

the hornbook and reread the letters. Soon
his eyes were again on the older pupils.

Suddenly the Quaker teacher snapped,
"Since thee has time to waste, Master
Banneker, let us hear the alphabet!"

Ben obeyed. In a shaking voice he read
every letter perfectly.

The teacher looked surprised. "That is
very good. Can thee read, Benjamin?"

"A little," said Ben modestly.

The teacher put a book into Ben's hands. "Let us hear thee."

The book was a primer for beginning readers. Ben found it much easier to read than the Bible. Even the older pupils listened to him in amazement.

The teacher said gruffly, "Thee may sit with the older class in reading, Benjamin."

In a few weeks Ben was also studying arithmetic with the advanced students. He liked numbers as much as he liked words.

As the years went by, he stayed at the head of his class. Soon his father turned to him whenever he had some figuring to do.

"How much seed should we buy for an acre of corn?" Robert would ask. "How much lumber will we need to enlarge the barn?"

Happily Ben would jot down figures. Usually he would find the right answer.

## 2.  The Last Day

Ben opened the back door quietly and strode down the path to the barn, swinging the empty milk pail. Of average size for his fifteen years, he was strong and a good worker.

No one else in the family was awake. The dew was still on the grass, and the air felt fresh and cool on his face. An oriole sang in the maple tree behind the house. Ben liked the early morning. It was a good time for thinking.

In the barn he sat down on the milking stool and rested his forehead against the cow's side as he milked her.

This was the last day of school before the summer vacation. Benjamin was sorry, for he enjoyed studying. Even during recess when the other pupils were playing in the yard, Ben had often stayed inside to read or work on a problem.

He had attended school for the past nine years. Not many boys, white or black, had that much education, but Ben wished he could continue school for another nine—another twenty-nine years! There were so many things he wanted to learn.

However, his father needed him on the farm. Even though Ben worked before and after school, it was not enough. With only a horse and plow and a few simple tools to help them, they had to do most of the work on the hundred-acre farm with their own hands.

Mary Banneker often reminded her son how fortunate they were to own so much land. Most of the black people in the American colonies were slaves who owned no land at all. She and Ben's father had bought the farm themselves, for a price of seven thousand pounds of tobacco.

By the time Ben returned from milking the cows, his mother and grandmother were preparing breakfast and his father was washing his hands and face in a basin.

"The last day of the term, isn't it, Ben?" asked his mother. She was stirring grits in a pot that hung over the fire in the fireplace.

Ben set the pail of milk on the table. "Yes," he said, "and I won't be going back in the fall."

His mother straightened up and studied his face with her alert brown eyes. Her pale copper-colored cheeks were reddened by the fire, and Ben thought, as he often did, how beautiful she was. She looked rather like an Indian with those thick black braids hanging over her shoulders.

"You've been quiet these past days," she said. "I knew you were working something out in your mind."

Benjamin's grandmother was filling pewter mugs with fresh, foamy milk from the pail. "Ben's just like his grandfather," she declared. "Bannaky was always one to think out his problems by himself, too. Ah, he was a fine man!" She paused, with the milk pail in her hand, her blue eyes staring into space.

Benjamin knew that his grandmother was remembering ...

When Ben's grandmother was a young girl, working on a dairy farm in England, she had been accused of stealing a pail of milk. Actually, the cow kicked the pail over, she had told Ben.

For this "crime" she was sent to America, and for seven years had to work for a tobacco farmer to pay for her passage. Whenever possible she had helped on other nearby farms to earn a little money.

At the end of the seven years she used the few dollars she had saved to buy a small farm in Maryland.

"The work was too much for me alone," Ben's grandmother had told him. "So I bought two African slaves from a ship that was anchored in Chesapeake Bay."

One of the slaves was Bannaky, the son of an African king. After a year or so Grandmother had set both slaves free and had married Bannaky. Ben's mother, Mary, was their daughter.

As Benjamin hurried down the trail toward school, he thought with pride of his grandfather who would have been a king if he had been able to stay in Africa. How glad he was that Bannaky's name had come down to him, even though now it was spelled Banneker. Ben's father was a freed slave, and like many slaves, he had no last name. So, when he married, he took his wife's last name, Banneker.

At school the teacher called Benjamin to his desk. "I have taught thee all I know of mathematics," he told him. "There's little more I can teach thee in any subject. But with thy good mind thee should learn a trade. I believe I can arrange for thee to be apprenticed to a printer I know in Baltimore."

For a moment Benjamin felt a surge of hope. He would like to go away where he would have a chance to learn more. "Thank you—thank you!" He tried to keep his voice steady as he added, "How I wish I could go to Baltimore, but I can't. I'm needed at home."

The teacher looked at him with understanding. "It's a pity, for thee is the best student I have ever had. This new land has need of men like thee." He led Ben to his bookshelf. "My books are thine to use, so choose some now to take home to study."

When Ben, with his arms full of books, said good-bye to his schoolmaster, there were tears in his teacher's eyes as well as in his own.

## 3. The Wooden Clock

On a winter evening when Benjamin Banneker was twenty-one, he sat down at the kitchen table as soon as the supper dishes were cleared.

In front of him he placed a piece of fine-grained hardwood and a pocket watch that he had borrowed from a friend.

Ben's mother pulled a chair close to the table so she could sew by the light of the candle, and his sister Minta leaned over his shoulder. Minta was a young woman, but she had never before had a chance to look closely at a watch. Few people in the American colonies had a watch or clock.

"How wonderful it would be to own that!" She touched the watch with one slim finger. "I could always know what time it is."

Holding the watch firmly in his left hand, Ben pried it open so he could see the busy wheels inside.

Minta gasped. "Should you do that? It isn't your watch."

Ben grinned at her. "Wait till you see what I'm going to do next. I'm going to take it apart. But don't worry. I have permission to do what I wish, as long as I put it together again."

Ben's father and his sister Molly joined the other members of the family around the table. Only Ben's married sister was missing. Outside, a cold wind whistled around the log cabin. Now and then the howl of a wolf or the cry of a bobcat could be heard. Inside the only sound was the crackling of the fire. One by one, Ben removed the tiny wheels and gears, carefully memorizing their arrangement in the watch as he placed them on the table.

He had forgotten anyone else was in the room with him. When his sister Molly spoke, he was startled.

"Why are you taking all the pieces out of the watch?" she asked.

Ben rubbed the back of his neck where it ached from bending over his work. "I'm going to make a clock," he announced. "I saw a picture of one in a book. I'm sure I can make one after I study this watch."

"A clock!" Ben's mother let her sewing drop into her lap. "How can you do that? You don't have any metal or the right tools."

Ben put one capable hand onto the piece of hardwood that lay on the table. "I have wood and a knife. I'll carve all the parts out of wood."

Several nights passed before he began to carve. First, he had to measure the wheels and figure out the size that each wheel in his clock should be. As he worked, he found he constantly needed his knowledge of mathematics.

Every night that winter he worked on his clock. When spring and summer came he had less free time, but whenever he could spare a moment from work on the farm he continued to figure and carve.

Patiently he fashioned the wheels with their toothed edges. Every piece must be exact. Often he would have a wheel almost complete and then a small slip of his knife would ruin it.

He would not use a spring in his clock.

A weighted cord wound around a spool would take its place. The clock must have a pendulum, too.

The neighbors for miles around learned of Benjamin's project and came to watch him. They knew that he was clever with his hands as well as with his mind. He was always making a piece of furniture or a tool. And look at the way he had taught himself to play the violin and the flute! But this time, surely, he was trying to do something that no one could do. To make a clock of wood, without another clock as a pattern, seemed impossible.

Even Benjamin was sometimes discouraged. After months of work he had the carefully carved parts in place. His wooden clock had begun to look like a clock, but a serious problem remained. He could not get the hour and minute hands to move together at the proper rate.

Again and again he studied the mechanism of the watch. Again and again he took his clock apart and put it together. A year had passed since he first started to make it.

"Why don't you give up?" asked his sister Minta. "It's a fine clock. What if one hand does run a little too fast?"

Benjamin set his lips more firmly together. "It must keep perfect time."

Several days later he discovered the error in his work and set it right. When at last he saw the hands of the clock working in harmony, he felt at peace.

He enclosed his clock in a neat case and hung it on the wall.

Day after day and year after year people came to see Benjamin Banneker's wooden clock that kept time accurately.

The borrowed watch, unharmed, was again in the pocket of its owner.

## 4. Let's Ask Banneker

It had been a hot day. Ben couldn't remember a hotter July.

After supper he dropped onto the front steps, too tired even to read. His mother sat on a bench, fanning herself. They had worked together in the fields all day. The tobacco was doing well and they had a fine vegetable garden. Their hives of bees supplied them with plenty of delicious honey and their cherry and pear trees were the best in the countryside.

Still Ben and his mother were sad tonight, for only two weeks earlier Ben's father had died. Benjamin had written in the Bible: "Robert Banneker departed this life July the 10th, 1759."

Ben, at twenty-seven, was now the head of the house. His three sisters were married and lived in their own cabins nearby. Ben never doubted that he should stay home and run the farm for his mother. He had not married, nor did he seem to have time for a social life. His work and his books kept him too busy.

Suddenly a loud BOOM brought Ben to his feet.

He and his mother knew that the boom of a cannon at sunset meant that one of the big plantations had received supplies from abroad. On the next day the owner would sell all that he did not need to neighboring farmers.

Ben's mother spoke up. "Now you can buy a new plow. I'll be glad to take care of the livestock tomorrow so you can get an early start."

The next morning Benjamin took the trail to the east, riding one of his horses and leading another. The second horse would carry his purchases home.

Down the hill he went, then across a valley, and soon he was climbing another small hill. As he rode through the thick forest, Ben surprised a deer. It leaped over the bushes as if it had wings and disappeared among the trees.

Part of his journey was over one of the "rolling roads." These roads were so named because farmers took their hogsheads, or barrels, of tobacco to market by rolling them over and over along them.

When Ben arrived at the plantation where the sale was being held, a crowd had already begun to gather. Several horses were tied to the fence, and slaves from the plantation were arranging the items to be sold on tables or on the grass in front of the white-pillared house.

Ben looked for the display of farm tools. Before he had time to select a new plow, someone shouted, "Banneker's here, Fred! Now's your chance!"

A plump white farmer, perspiring in the heat, hurried across the grass. "Ben!" he puffed. "You're the very man I want to see. I need your help with a problem. I'm building a corncrib, and I don't know how large to make it. All I know is I want it to hold about 200 bushels of corn."

Benjamin smiled. "I'll be glad to help you." He was accustomed to such questions, and he enjoyed answering them. Neighbors had learned that Benjamin Banneker could solve almost any problem in mathematics. In a short time he told the farmer how large the corncrib should be.

Ben bought a plow and some seed. Then, seeing a table covered with bolts of cloth, he selected a fine, soft, brown material for a dress for his mother.

For himself, he bought a copy of a book by the Greek thinker Plato. He and his mother were not wealthy like the plantation owners, thought Ben, but they had enough. Few small farmers in the area, white or black, were more comfortable than the Bannekers.

Also the Bannekers were free. Not many black people had their freedom, and this was a constant worry to Banneker. He often wondered what he could do to help his enslaved brothers.

Several men were having a lively conversation about the tax money Britain was taking from her colonies in America. They asked Ben what he thought and listened respectfully to his answer, for

Ben was always well informed. There were few things Banneker liked more than an interesting discussion, but he was modest and rarely gave his opinion unless it was asked.

Soon he excused himself, for he had much work to do, and he hoped to find time that night to read from his new book. Also, he thought longingly of his violin and flute. He loved to play them, but he rarely managed to save more than a half hour at twilight for music.

On the way home he thought of the people with whom he had talked that day. All had been friendly, and yet he did not have much in common with any of them. He wished he had a friend who shared his interests.

Banneker's busy life did not leave him much time to feel sorry for himself, but today he realized he was often lonely.

## 5. Important Visitors

Benjamin Banneker caught a glimpse of the men climbing the hill and pointed them out to his mother.

"Look, I believe some of the Ellicotts are coming to visit us."

Mary Banneker was on her hands and knees beside a huge hickory tree, digging up a small plant. It was a fine Sunday in May, a good day to be outdoors. She was looking for the healing herbs from which she made medicines to help the sick.

Jumping to her feet, Mary stared down the trail. "You're right!" she exclaimed. "I'll go put the kettle on." Although she was nearing sixty, Mary snatched up her bag of herbs and ran up the path like a young girl.

Benjamin walked down the trail to meet the visitors. There were two men and a boy, and, as they drew nearer, he recognized the brothers John and Andrew Ellicott. Andrew's son George, a boy of about twelve, was with them.

"Well met, Mr. Banneker!" one of the men called out. "We were on our way to see you."

Benjamin smiled. "I'm honored, indeed, Mr. Ellicott."

Benjamin was pleased to be called Mr. Banneker. Few white people called a black man *mister*. The Ellicotts were Quakers and, like most people who were

of that faith, they believed in treating all men as brothers.

John and Andrew Ellicott and two other brothers had recently come all the way from Pennsylvania to build mills on the Patapsco River just ten miles west of Baltimore and only a mile from Benjamin's house. They had brought with them all the machinery for the mills—much of it of their own design. They had traveled by boat as far as Elk Ridge Landing on the Patapsco. From this point on, the river was impossible to navigate. Not even a rough road led to the valley several miles upstream where they wished to build their mills. Therefore they had taken their machinery and wagons apart and had carried them overland, piece by piece. As soon as the men arrived, they began to clear the land and to build a dam and a bridge across the river.

Already the people in the area admired the Ellicotts.

Inside the Banneker house John and Andrew Ellicott sat at the table drinking tea while young George drank a cup of milk and ate several of the little cakes Mary had set out. Remembering his own youth, Ben had put the plate of cakes near George. He noticed that the boy seemed to follow the men's conversation with interest.

Ben was a courteous host, forgetting his usual shyness in making sure his visitors were comfortable. He was unaware that his guests were admiring his good-looking, brown-skinned face, his broad forehead, and gentle, thoughtful eyes.

"We've heard so much about your clock, we had to come to see it," said John Ellicott.

"Of course." Benjamin started to rise.

John held out his hand. "But first we'd like to talk over a business matter."

As Ben sat down he noticed that George looked disappointed.

John continued. "This is our problem. We need fresh vegetables and milk for our families and workmen. Could you supply us?"

Mary Banneker spoke up. "That we can, and gladly. Besides, Ben has good honey from his bees, and I can bring you fresh eggs and chickens for your table."

"Wonderful!" John Ellicott beamed at Ben and his mother.

Ben chuckled. "Some day you must come up and watch my mother catch a chicken for market. The poor bird hasn't a chance once she sets after it. She chases it till it surrenders."

The men smiled at Mrs. Banneker. Then Andrew brought the discussion back to business. "Mr. Banneker, I notice you and all the other farmers around here plant a great deal of tobacco."

"Yes," said Ben, "it's been our chief crop for years."

Andrew Ellicott pushed back his teacup. "We're building a flour mill and we're going to need wheat. We've planted some, but we'll need much more than we can grow. If you'll plant your acres in wheat, we'll buy it from you. You'll make more from it than from tobacco. Will you try it?"

Benjamin met Andrew's steady gaze. This was a man who inspired confidence. Besides, Ben knew that tobacco was taking the richness out of the soil. "Yes," he agreed, "I'll put in wheat at my next planting."

Young George glanced at Ben's clock which hung on the wall at the end of

the room. He said quietly to his father, "The clock—don't forget the clock."

Benjamin heard him, and taking the clock from the wall, he brought it to the table. "Here it is, Master George."

George looked at the clock eagerly.

Benjamin opened the case to show him the wooden works ·inside. "I finished it nineteen years ago, when I was twenty-two. I had a terrible time getting it to run properly."

46

George was too fascinated to say a word.

"It's amazing!" said Andrew.

John Ellicott looked earnestly at Ben. "I understand you had never seen a clock when you made this one."

"I had a borrowed watch."

"But that was quite different. Your clock doesn't operate the same as a watch." John motioned to the clock on the table. "From what I hear, this is as original as if you had invented clocks. What a mind you must have!"

"Thank you, sir." Ben busied himself with closing the clock case.

"My Uncle Joseph made a clock," volunteered George.

Andrew put his hand on George's shoulder. "Yes, he and his son Andrew—our family is full of Andrews—made it. We're all proud of that clock, but I'm sure that what you did, Mr. Banneker, was harder. They had metal to use, and all kinds of tools. You must see Joseph's clock, though. It has four sides, and it shows the planets in orbit and the changes of the moon."

"And it plays tunes," said George. "Twenty-four different tunes. On one side there's a window where you can see the inside—"

Ben enjoyed the boy's enthusiasm, but Andrew seemed to think his son was talking too much. "Enough, George," he said, "Mr. Banneker must see it for himself."

Benjamin's dark eyes shone. "I should like to," he answered. Suddenly his world was widening. These men with their many fields of knowledge were going to live nearby, and they seemed to want to be friends.

## 6. Ben Discovers Astronomy

One morning Benjamin was cleaning out the spring that rose beneath a golden willow tree in the middle of his orchard. It gave a steady flow of pure water that Ben used for drinking, to water his cattle and horses, and for all the needs of his farm.

He was so busy he did not hear the hoofbeats approaching on the dirt road until they slowed down near his house.

Drying his hands on his work smock, he hurried up the hill. In his yard he saw the familiar figure of George Ellicott, now a tall, good-looking man of twenty-seven. He and his father and uncles had long been friends of Banneker. Their friendship had changed Ben's life. The Ellicotts loaned him books and often came to visit him. They had taught him surveying. When they had distinguished visitors they invited Ben to meet them. In return, he helped them in countless ways.

The mills built by the Ellicotts were doing well. They used all the wheat that the farmers for miles around could grow. Ellicott's Mills were becoming famous for the flour they turned out. Much of it went to Baltimore over a road George Ellicott had surveyed when he was only seventeen. From there the flour was shipped to England and other countries.

George was a capable young man. Besides being a surveyor, he also was a fine mathematician and astronomer. In spite of the differences in age and color, he and Benjamin were warm friends.

"I have something I think will interest you!" George called out. He leaped down from his horse and opened one of the saddlebags. From it he took three books which he gave to Benjamin. From the other bag he pulled several instruments, one of which Benjamin recognized as a telescope.

"I've studied these books on astronomy until I almost know them by heart," said George. "You may keep them as long as you like." He set the telescope and other instruments in the house. "I wish I could stay to explain how these work, but I'm in a hurry. I have to go away on business." He added with a laugh, "When I come back I'll be your teacher." The two took turns being teacher—depending on which one knew more about a subject.

Although it was mid-morning, and he had work to do, Benjamin could not resist glancing at the books. He sat down on his doorstep and opened the first, which happened to be Ferguson's *Astronomy*.

When his clock struck noon it surprised Ben. The rest of that day he rushed through the farm work, trying to make up for lost time.

That evening Ben returned to the books, and found the other two—Mayer's *Tables* and Leadbetter's *Lunar Tables*—just as absorbing as the first book. They were hard to understand, though, for the study of astronomy requires a knowledge of advanced mathematics. Much of the work in these books was new to Ben, but he would not give up.

On and on he studied. When it was completely dark, he set up the telescope

on a table near an open window and trained it on the stars. Then he returned to read more by the light of a candle. At times he went outdoors and lay on his back on the ground, staring at the sky. Back and forth he went all night, reading about the stars and looking at them.

At last he closed the books. It was morning and time to milk the cows.

When George Ellicott returned from his business trip, he was clearly amazed at Banneker's progress. "I don't see how you've gone so far without help. You're a genius!"

Benjamin said in his gentle way, "I fear my neighbors think I have lost my mind or else that I've become lazy. I stay up all night, and they find me asleep at noon!"

Benjamin had found the love of his life —astronomy. From this time on, it was his chief interest. As he continued his study, he even found errors made by Ferguson and Leadbetter, the famous astronomers whose books he used. In 1789, only two years after he had first received the books on astronomy, he correctly predicted an eclipse of the sun.

"You should make an almanac," suggested George Ellicott. An almanac was the one scientific work to be found in almost every home. Farmers studied it to find out when to plant their crops. Seafaring men turned to it to learn about ocean tides. Women read it for recipes and advice on care of the sick.

"I couldn't!" protested Ben. Producing such a book, he thought, was not a task for a man with so little education.

Still the idea appealed to Banneker. Some day he would surely follow George's suggestion.

# 7. Time for Science

One day just before lunch, Benjamin heard a knock on his door. Laying down his pen, he went to admit his visitor.

Three boys were standing there. One stepped forward and asked politely, "Mr. Banneker, may we pick some pears?"

Ben sighed. He knew these boys well. They had come earlier in the year to ask if they might have some of the cherries from his trees. He had given them permission to take some, but while he was deep in his work, they had stripped the trees, leaving no fruit for him.

Banneker was not the kind of person who could shout at the boys or try to frighten them into leaving his orchard alone. He could only reason with them.

He said quietly, "I don't mind if you take some pears for your own use, but I must sell the fruits and vegetables I raise if I am to live."

"Yes, Mr. Banneker," they answered in a chorus. "Thank you, sir."

Their words were polite, but Ben saw the mischief in their eyes. Well, he couldn't stand outside and watch them. He had too much work to do.

That afternoon he was glad to see that the fruit still hung thick and heavy on the pear trees. Tomorrow morning, he thought, he would pick all the ripe pears to sell to the workers at the mills. He would put aside baskets for his sisters and for his friend George Ellicott.

However, the next morning when he went to his orchard, the pears were gone. Leaves and broken branches littered the ground. The thieves had been in a hurry.

Ben went sadly from tree to tree picking the few pears the boys had missed. When he finished he had only a half bushel of pears.

When had the boys picked his fruit?— last evening while he worked on some mathematical problems—or in the night when he was studying the sky?

Downhearted, he returned to his log house. This last blow made him decide on a plan he had long considered. He would turn over his land to the Ellicotts in return for a yearly sum of money. That way he would have enough to live on, and he would be free to work on mathematics and astronomy and to pursue his other interests.

After doing some figuring at his oval table, he put on a suit of unbleached linen, freshly laundered by one of his sisters. As he buttoned the coat over his rather stout body, his thoughts turned to the care with which Minta and Molly looked after his needs.

He picked up the paper on which he had done his figuring and then set off down the road to Ellicott's Mills. There he had a long talk with George Ellicott and his brothers, Jonathan and Elias.

"I consider my land is worth one hundred eighty pounds," he said. "I believe I shall live fifteen years. If you will pay me twelve pounds a year for fifteen years, I will receive the full value of the land."

"What if you die before that time?" asked George.

"In that case, you will own my land more quickly."

The Ellicotts agreed to the plan.

Ben had a new lightness in his step as he climbed the hill. Now he was free to work on the studies he enjoyed. He need no longer depend on the fruits of his land for a living. Twelve pounds each year amounted to about thirty-two dollars, and that was enough for his simple wants. He would continue to care for a little garden, but he would raise only enough for his own use. Of course he would look after the fruit trees. Perhaps when the boys learned the Ellicotts were now the real owners of his land, they would not take his fruit.

He was sorry not to leave his land to his relatives, but it would not amount to much if it were divided among all of them. They would understand.

That evening after supper he sat for a long time under one of the stripped pear trees, playing his violin. His sister Minta and some of his nephews and nieces came to listen. As he looked at their loving faces, he felt that he was a fortunate man.

Even though he was now freed from making a living, Ben was constantly busy. He studied his bees and wrote a paper about their habits. He thought about the locusts—grasshopperlike insects that sometimes appeared suddenly and ate the crops.

One day when his sister Molly arrived with clean clothes she had washed and ironed for him, Benjamin announced, "I believe I can predict that locusts will next come to feast on our crops in 1800."

Molly was surprised, because no one ever knew when to expect the dreaded locusts. However, she knew Ben would not make such a statement if it were not based on facts.

"How can you tell that?" she asked.

"I have discovered that they come every seventeen years," he said. "Listen. I've written down some of my observations." He read aloud:

The first great locust year that I remember was in 1749. I was then about seventeen years old, when thousands of them came and were creeping about the bushes. I then imagined they came to eat and destroy the fruit of the earth, and would occasion a famine in the land. I therefore began to kill and destroy them, but soon saw that the labor was in vain, and therefore gave over my pretension. Again in the year 1766, which is seventeen years after their first appearance to me, they made a second, and appeared to me as numerous . . .

Again in the year 1783, which was seventeen years from their second appearance to me, they made their third, and may be expected again in 1800, which is seventeen years since their third appearance to me. So that I may venture to express it, their periodical return is seventeen years; but they, like the comets, make a short stay with us.

Molly's dark eyes were full of admiration for her brother. "I don't know how you think of these things, Ben." She chuckled. "If Grandma were alive, she'd say, 'You're just like Bannaky.'"

Molly got up to go. "I must go home and tell my husband about the locusts."

When Molly had left, Ben had an idea for a mathematical problem that would amuse his friend George Ellicott. He began to write it in verse:

*A cooper and vintner sat down for a talk,*
*Both being so groggy that neither could walk;*
*Says cooper to vintner, "I'm the first of my trade,*
*There's no kind of vessel but what I have made,*
*And of any shape, sir, just what you will,*
*And of any size, sir, from a tun to a gill."*

Ben smiled to himself as he continued to make up the problem. George would have trouble solving this one.

Mathematical puzzles in verse were fun, but a more serious project occupied most of Banneker's time. He began to work on an almanac for the year 1791—to see if he could do it. Carefully he figured out the phases of the moon, the times for the rise and fall of the tides, and the positions of the planets. When at last his almanac was complete, he was quite

pleased with it. It was some time before
he showed it to George Ellicott.

"It's excellent," George said. "I just wish
I had seen this sooner. It's too late now
to have it printed. All the same, I'd like
to show it to some friends. Will you do
another for 1792? I feel sure we can find
a publisher."

Happily, Benjamin agreed. Imagine people reading his almanac!

## 8. Ben Helps to Plan a City

A raw wind whipped at Banneker's coat as he rode down the hill to the post office. In spite of the cold, he was determined to pick up his mail. Who could say what he might receive?—perhaps a letter with a problem for him to solve or a book he had ordered from England.

As Ben tied his horse to the rail in front of the combination post office and general store, Andrew Ellicott came down the steps of the building. He was the same Andrew who years before had helped his father make the clock with four sides.

He came directly to Benjamin and shook hands with him, saying, "Come inside where it's warm. I have something I want to ask you."

Andrew led the way to a tiny office behind the counter. He came at once to the point.

"Ben, do you know that President Washington plans to build a new federal city on the Potomac?"

Benjamin nodded. "Yes, and I know that he wisely put you in charge of surveying the territory."

Ben knew that the new federal city was to be located on the Potomac River, between Maryland and Virginia. Both states had given land for the purpose. In time, President Washington and the other members of the federal government would move there from New York City where they now met. They would have to wait, though. As yet, the federal city was only a wilderness. The president had appointed several commissioners to direct the survey of the ten square miles of land and the laying out of the streets of the future city.

Now Andrew leaned forward excitedly. "Would you be willing to work with me? I'd like to name you as my assistant."

The site for the federal city looked like this when Banneker helped survey it.

Ben looked doubtful. "You're joking!"

"Not for a minute. I want you to work with me. Your knowledge of astronomy will be useful, and I need someone to help with the observations."

Benjamin smiled. "I feel safe in saying yes." He was sure he would not be accepted. Still, he could not help dreaming. If his appointment were approved, he then might meet such men as Thomas Jefferson. Perhaps he might even see the president, George Washington! Firmly, Banneker put the matter out of his mind. It was no use thinking of something so wonderful—and unlikely.

In the meantime, George Ellicott had found a printer who was interested in Benjamin's almanac. If Banneker would prepare an almanac for the year 1792, they—Goddard and Angell, Publishers, of Baltimore—would print it.

Benjamin gladly accepted their offer.

Then Andrew Ellicott came to him with news. "I've talked with Thomas Jefferson. It's settled," he said. "You're to work for me on the survey of the federal territory."

Ben was amazed. "I *never* expected it!" he gasped. "I've agreed to calculate an almanac for 1792."

"The survey of our nation's capital must come first," said Andrew solemnly. "I'm sure you'll still have time to do the almanac when you return."

Ben took a deep breath. "I'll try."

In February 1791, Benjamin set out on horseback on the more than forty-mile trip to the federal territory. As he rode, he wondered how he would be accepted by the other men who were helping with the survey. They might be different from the Ellicotts, who never seemed to care that his skin was black. Ben had even heard that Secretary of State Thomas Jefferson, who had agreed to his employment, did not believe black men were mentally the equal of white.

However, Ben need not have worried. His intelligence and good manners quickly won the admiration and respect of the men with whom he worked. He sat with them during conferences. He lodged with them, and they urged him to eat at their table. This he refused, since it was not the custom for black people and white to eat together. Instead, he sat at a separate table in the same room.

The rough, wooded square of land where the surveyors began work did not look like the site of a city. Hundreds of trees had to be cut down before they could even start the survey. The men had to fight insects, snakes, swamp holes, and a dense tangle of trees and climbing vines. In spite of this, to Ben the survey was better than play. He was doing work he liked with men whose company he enjoyed.

First, he and Ellicott laid out the boundary lines of the ten-mile square. Then they plotted a true north-south line. Just as Andrew had planned, they used

their knowledge of astronomy to make this line accurate. When the north-south line was located, they crossed it with one going east and west. The capitol would be built at the point where these lines crossed. Soon the survey of the sites of the capitol and the president's house was begun. The surveying team was making good progress.

Within a short time everyone connected with the project found out that Major L'Enfant, the French engineer who was in charge of planning the city, was a hot-tempered man.

His plans for the city were brilliant. Banneker and Ellicott agreed on that, as did many others. Yet the plans were not always practical. Besides, the Frenchman refused to follow the directions given by the commissioners.

Andrew Ellicott and Ben worried about this problem. L'Enfant's actions affected the progress of their own work.

Ben wished he could stay to see the completion of the survey and planning, but he knew he must go home before summer if he were to complete his almanac in time for the printer.

At home Benjamin's sisters and young nephews and nieces were eager to hear about his experiences. They watched him draw a map of the city in the dust with a stick.

"See, the capitol will be the center of the city. The streets will go out from it like the spokes of a wheel. Like this."

The children leaned over the map Ben had drawn. They tried to imagine how the city would look.

"The streets will be wider than any you have ever seen," Benjamin explained. "The important streets will be as much as one hundred sixty feet wide. They'll be divided into footways and rows of trees and a carriage way."

It would be a beautiful city, thought Benjamin. As he returned to his lonely house, he wished his mother were alive so he could tell her all about it.

Still, the problems were continuing at the site of the federal city. In March of

Banneker's good friend
Andrew Ellicott, at left,
drew this plan of the
city of Washington.

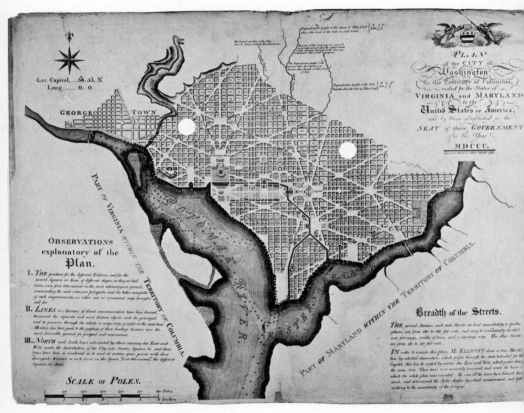

the following year the president dismissed L'Enfant. He left angrily, taking his plans with him. Washington put Andrew Ellicott in charge of completing the work. Now, besides doing the survey, he had to design and map the city and choose locations for all the public buildings.

On his occasional trips home he often discussed his work with Benjamin.

"I want to use as many of L'Enfant's ideas as possible," he told Ben.

When Ellicott drew up the map of the city, it contained most of the good features of L'Enfant's plans, plus necessary changes. George Washington was delighted.

## 9. Maker of Almanacs

It was a hot night. The call of the whippoorwill came through the open windows. Mosquitoes, attracted by the light of the candle, buzzed around Banneker's head. Wearily he brushed them away. Without raising his eyes from the paper before him, he dipped his quill pen into the ink to write another line.

The oval table that stood in the main room of his log cabin was strewn with papers. Ben was making a copy of his almanac to send to the printers. Every number and word must be correct. When at last he finished, he stood up and stretched and ran his fingers through his thick grey curls. He had had to work long hours to finish the almanac in time, and he was glad it was done.

Stepping outside, he looked up at the stars. They were so familiar to him they seemed like old friends. Tonight he was too tired to study them. He must rest because tomorrow he wanted to make another copy of his almanac.

He had thought of something he could do to help other black people. He would send a copy of his almanac to Thomas Jefferson. When Jefferson saw what one black man could do, perhaps it would help to change his opinion of all black men. Jefferson had already tried to put a stop to the importing of slaves. Ben hoped he could be persuaded to do even more.

The next day Banneker made another neat copy of the almanac. Then he wrote a letter to accompany it. He began:

MARYLAND, BALTIMORE COUNTY,
NEAR ELLICOTT'S LOWER MILLS,
August 19th, 1791
To Thomas Jefferson,
Secretary of State, Philadelphia

SIR.—I am fully sensible of the greatness of that freedom which I take on the present occasion; a liberty, which seemed to me scarcely allowable, when I reflected on that distinguished and honorable station in which you stand; and, the almost general prejudice and prepossession which is prevalent in the world, against those of my complexion.

As Benjamin continued the letter, he reminded Jefferson of the recent war that had been fought to free the colonies from England. He quoted those words that Jefferson, himself, had written in the Declaration of Independence:

> We hold these truths to be self-evident, that all men are created equal, and that they are endowed by their Creator with certain inalienable rights, that amongst these are Life, Liberty, and the pursuit of Happiness.

The same liberty, Banneker said, should be given to all men, regardless of their color. He urged Jefferson to do all in his power to set the slaves free.

Thomas Jefferson replied warmly to Ben's letter, saying that he wished as soon as possible to see the condition of the Negroes improved. He said he was sending the almanac to the secretary of

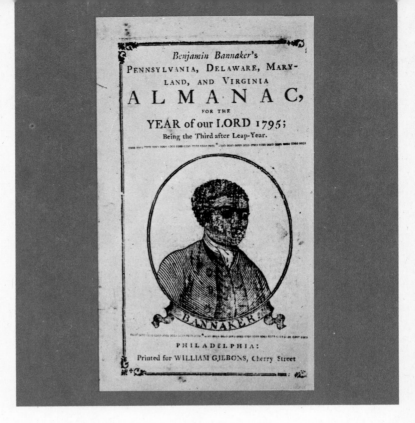

One issue of the popular *Almanac* included
a woodcut portrait of Ben.

the Academy of Sciences in Paris because
it was a credit to all men of Banneker's
color.

When Banneker's *Almanac for 1792* was
published, it contained a letter written to
the publishers by James McHenry. He
was a distinguished man who had served

84

in the Maryland Senate and had been a delegate to the Constitutional Convention. He later became secretary of war under President Adams.

Mr. McHenry praised the almanac and stated in the letter:

> I consider this Negro as a fresh proof that the powers of the mind are disconnected with the color of the skin.

For himself, Banneker did not seek praise. However, he was glad that his work made people realize that black men had the same abilities as white.

The almanac was the first of several, for Ben published one each year until 1797. People liked to read them. Besides scientific information, they contained poems and essays that Banneker had read and enjoyed. One gave a census of the states.

Another included an account of a yellow fever epidemic in Philadelphia.

Banneker's *Almanac for 1793* contained a plan for a peace office for the United States which had recently been proposed by Dr. Benjamin Rush. It suggested that a secretary of peace be appointed to help bring about world peace. One of his duties would be to "establish and maintain free schools in every city, village, and township in the United States." The peace office, the plan declared, should "inspire a veneration for human life, and an horror of the shedding of human blood."

Ben included this plan in his almanac to arouse his readers' interest in peace. As always, his mind was reaching out, searching for ways to help all people.

## 10. Worth More than Gold

One fine Sunday morning Banneker set out for a walk to enjoy the sunshine and look at the beauties of the countryside. It was October 9, 1806. Ben's seventy-fifth birthday was only a month away.

Though he stood proudly erect, he carried a staff to keep from falling. Years of hard work and of lying on the ground at night studying the stars had left him stiff and unsure of his legs.

Today, since it was Sunday and a cool day, he wore a fine broadcloth suit with a long jacket. On his head was a broad-brimmed beaver hat.

Here I am, still walking around, he thought with a feeling of wonder. Already Benjamin had lived well past the time he had expected to live. He was grateful to the Ellicotts who continued to pay the twelve pounds a year. They said his property had gone up in value so it was only right that they pay him more for it. That was true, but it was kind of them all the same.

A few years ago he had been so ill he had thought he was going to die. Then he had told his sisters what to do with all of his possessions.

Recently he had given one of his sisters a feather bed which he no longer needed. To which sister had he given it? He couldn't remember. That was strange. He stopped in the path and rubbed his eyes, because suddenly the autumn leaves had become blurred.

In a moment he could see again and he walked on rather slowly—a heavy, white-haired man with a long staff. Someone had said he looked like a black Benjamin Franklin.

How beautiful it was today! He had always enjoyed nature, but this day had a special glory. The sun brought out the brightness of the red and gold and green of the hills.

Behind him footsteps rustled the fallen leaves, and a moment later a friendly voice said, "Hello, Benjamin. What a beautiful day! May I join you?"

"Delighted," said Ben. He was happy to have a companion, though he only knew this man slightly.

As they strolled together, suddenly Benjamin felt sick. He stopped, thinking the weakness would go away, but it did not.

"I—I'll have to go back," he said in a faltering voice.

The man seemed to understand at once and took Benjamin's arm. At the house Ben went directly to the couch and lay down with a great feeling of relief. He closed his eyes and the world drifted away. In a few minutes the quiet inner hum of his life ceased.

The man with whom he had shared his last walk ran to call Ben's sisters and a doctor.

That very day Minta and Molly carried out their brother's wishes.

One of their sons drove a cart up to Benjamin's log house and, with the help of the entire family, loaded onto it the oval table at which Banneker had worked for years. His scientific instruments and books went onto the wagon and so did the manuscripts of his almanacs and letters. Then, slowly and sadly, his nephew drove the cart with its load of treasure to George Ellicott's home. With it he brought the unhappy news of Banneker's death.

Ben had left everything else he owned to his sisters, Minta Black and Molly Morton. They did take his Bible that day, but decided to wait until after the funeral to take the rest of their brother's possessions.

Two days later, during his funeral, Banneker's house burned to the ground. His clock was one of the valuable items lost in the flames. If his sisters had not sent his manuscripts and other papers to George Ellicott immediately, those possessions too would have been lost to mankind.

Years later Ben's sister to whom he had given his feather bed found in it a purse of gold coins. She always wondered if he had forgotten it was there or if he had left it as a surprise for her.

*The Federal Gazette and Baltimore Daily Advertiser* carried an article about

Banneker on Tuesday morning, October 28, 1806:

On Sunday, the 9th instant, departed this life, at his residence in Baltimore County, Mr. Benjamin Banneker, a black man, and immediate descendent of an African father. He was well known in his neighborhood for his quiet and peaceful demeanor, and, among scientific men, as an astronomer and mathematician.

In early life he was instructed in the most common rules of arithmetic, and thereafter, with the assistance of different authors, he was enabled to acquire a perfect knowledge of all the higher branches of learning. Mr. Banneker was the calculator of several almanacs, published in this as well as several of the neighboring States; and, although of late years none of his almanacs have been published, yet he never failed to calculate one every year, and left them among his papers. . . .

Mr. Banneker is a prominent instance to prove that a descendent of Africa is susceptible of as great mental improvement and deep knowledge of the mysteries of nature as that of any other nation.

Banneker spoke for his people with both words and accomplishments. His good and useful life moved all men nearer to mutual respect and understanding.

# Index